The Wreck of the Ten Sail

A true story from Cayman's past

Sam Oakley

ISBN HB 978-0-9576461-7-9
ISBN 978-0-9957368-0-1

A catalogue record for this book is available from the British Library

Published in Great Britain
in 2017 by
Polperro Heritage Press
Clifton-upon-Teme, Worcestershire WR6 6DH
United Kingdom
www.polperropress.co.uk

Printed by Orphans Press
Leominster HR6 0LD
United Kingdom

Maritime Heritage Trail
CAYMAN ISLANDS
Wreck of the Ten Sail

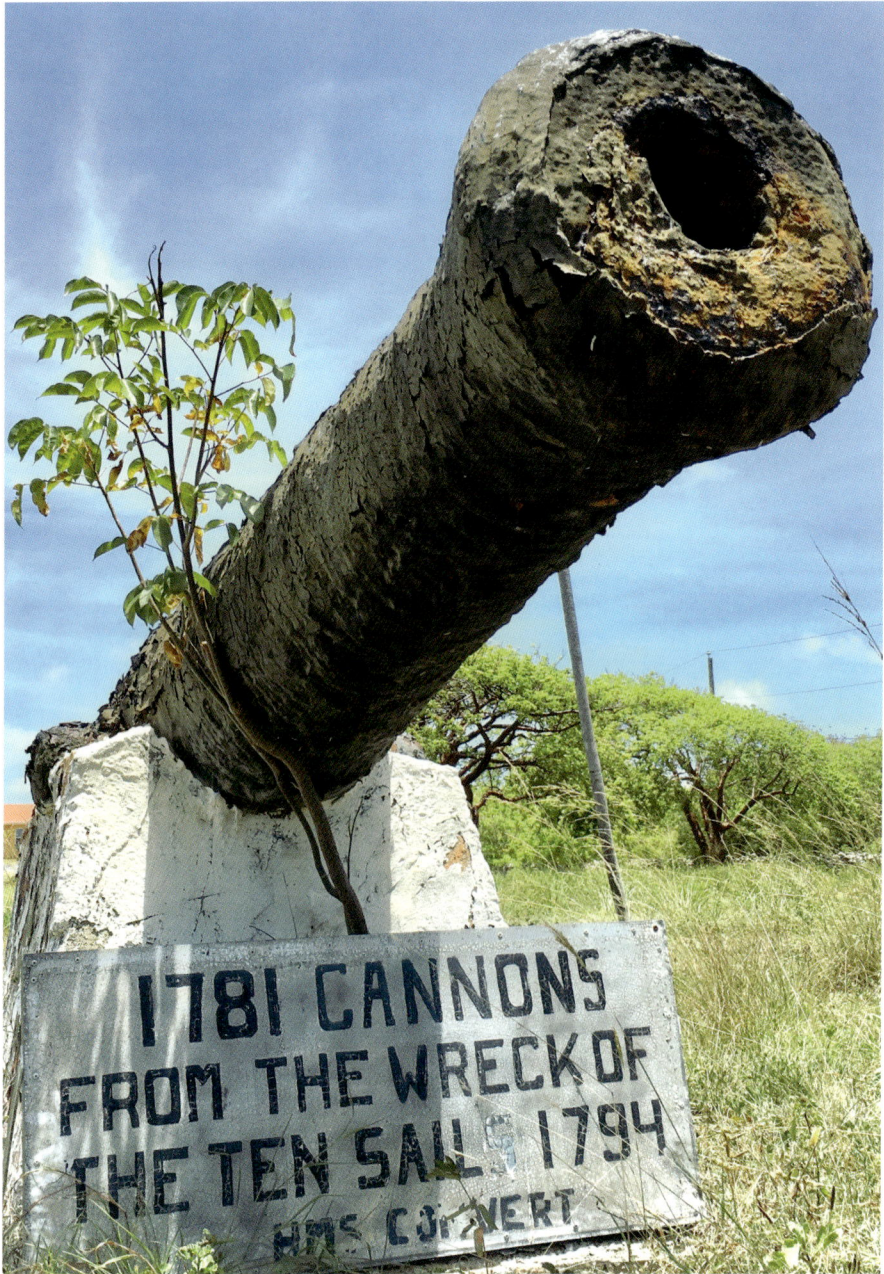

1781 CANNONS
FROM THE WRECK OF
THE TEN SAILS 1794
HMS CONVERT

Contents

36-gun fifth-rate frigate c1793 similar to HMS Convert

Introduction

The coral reefs surrounding the rugged coastlines of the Cayman Islands often, in times past, brought grief to ships voyaging in the Western Caribbean. Towards the end of the eighteenth century, hostilities between Britain and France during the French Revolutionary Wars extended to the West Indian seas with each country endeavouring to capture the other's naval ships and merchantmen as prizes.

In February 1794, His Majesty's ship *Convert*, a 36-gun frigate seized from the French the previous year, was charged with escorting and protecting a produce-laden convoy of merchant vessels to Britain from Jamaica. Ironically the greatest danger was to come not from the French but from the perilous eastern reefs of Grand Cayman where on 8th February 1794 a disastrous chain of events resulted in the loss of the *Convert* and nine ships of her merchant convoy. The inhabitants of Grand Cayman displayed considerable heroism in assisting in the rescue of more than 400 survivors and thanks to their bravery, few lives were lost.

Legend has long persisted that a British prince was among those rescued and that King George III granted the Cayman Islands its present tax advantageous status in gratitude for the islanders' efforts. While most modern historians have refuted such a claim, more recently evidence has emerged of a royal connection among the *Convert*'s rescued passengers.

The *Wreck of the Ten Sail* is a true story of Cayman's past that also reveals much of the Islands' history and character that has shaped the thriving economy that exists there today.

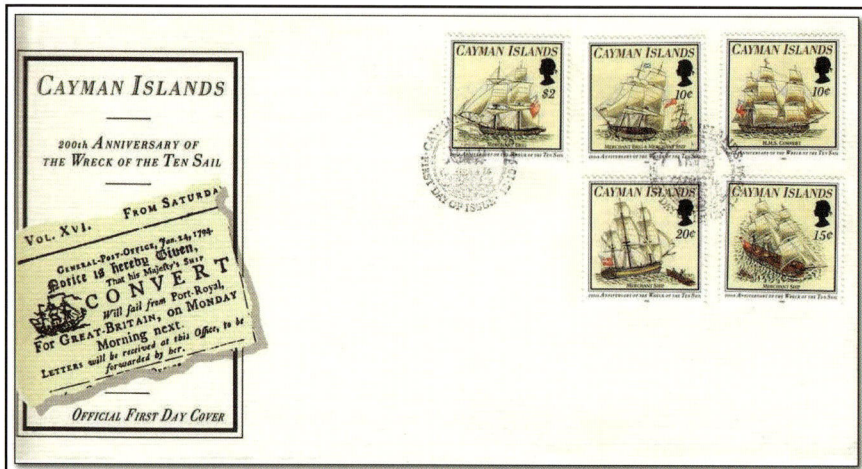

Early History

The first recorded mention of the Cayman Islands dates back to May 1503 when Christopher Columbus's son Ferdinand noted in his journal: 'We were in sight of two small low islands filled with tortoises, as was the sea all about'. Columbus named the islands Las Tortugas after the huge number of sea turtles he saw along the island's uninhabited shore.

Another early visitor was Sir Francis Drake who, in 1586, reported seeing 'great serpents called caimanas, like large lizards, which are edible'. It was the Islands' ample supply of turtle, however, that made them a popular calling place for ships sailing the Caribbean in need of meat for their crews.

The islands remained largely uninhabited until the 17th century. The first known settlers arrived around 1658, probably deserters from Oliver Cromwell's army in the West Indies. Many of the early inhabitants were also Britons from Jamaica and others were believed to be pirates that settled down looking for a more peaceful life. Britain took possession of the Cayman Islands and Jamaica following the Treaty of Madrid in 1670. Isaac Bodden, the first recorded permanent inhabitant of the

Cayman Islands, was born on Grand Cayman around 1700, the grandson of one of the original settlers named Bodden. Soon turtle fishermen, slaves, shipwrecked sailors, and refugees from the Spanish Inquisition joined the blend. The melting pot of cultures and backgrounds mixed together to create what we know as Cayman today.

Pirates

After Britain took possession of the Cayman Islands from the Spanish in 1670, most of the three islands were left untouched apart from small settlements on Grand Cayman and Little Cayman. This was ideal for pirates, since Cayman also lay astride the route of treasure galleons returning to Spain, laden with gold and silver from the New World.

The promise of capturing Spanish treasure ships on their way home from the Caribbean soon attracted the attention of a motley crowd of buccaneers, pirates and freebooters. The 'Golden Age' of piracy spanned from the 1650s to the 1730s and Cayman's most notorious pirate was Edward Teach, otherwise known as Blackbeard, who frequented the area from 1713 to his death in November 1718.

The Islands offered pirate captains the possibility of finding crews to man captured vessels and a quiet location away from the authorities where pirates could hide their loot and careen and repair their vessels. By the 1730s the scourge of piracy had been largely tamed, if not actively discouraged by the growing population.

Hurricanes

When Grand Cayman was hit by a devastating hurricane in October 1793 the islands were battered and pounded by the sea, the relentless winds destroying homes and livelihoods in an instant.

The vast majority of homes on the island at the time were simple shacks made of wooden frames and thatched with the local silver palm. These thatch-work buildings were relatively quick to assemble but unfortunately even quicker to be destroyed during a heavy storm.

1793, 20th and 21st October
The West End of the island was overflowed by the sea, and several houses were washed away. At Boatswain's bay, every house was destroyed. The plantain walks and provision grounds, in general, are desolated, and such was the violence of the tempest, that the cocoa- nut trees were torn out by the roots. The inhabitants are in great distress for provisions, from this calamity, and look up to Jamaica for relief.

The Royal Gazette, 21st December 1793

This part of the Caribbean is one of the world's most hurricane active areas. Since records began in 1871 over 85 tropical storms or hurricanes have affected the Cayman Islands. The Atlantic Basin hurricane season is from June 1st to the end of November, peaking between August and October when the waters are at their warmest.

The most recent hurricane to affect Grand Cayman was Hurricane Ivan in 2004. This was one of the most powerful hurricanes to hit the Caribbean in recorded history. The eye passed 21 miles south-west of Grand Cayman with winds of 150 mph and gusts of 220 mph. Incredibly only two people were reported dead. However 402 people were treated for lacerations, wounds, removal of foreign bodies, fractures and burns as a result of the disaster. There was no electricity, mains water and access to telecommunications for several days immediately after the storm.

Cayman c1794

Even before the hurricane had wreaked its devastation in October 1793, just four months before the Wreck of the Ten Sail, Grand Cayman could not be described as a lush and fertile place. 76 square miles - 22 miles long and an average of four miles wide, with no lakes or rivers, it was not well suited to growing much in the way of crops. At the time, about one third of the island was farmable land. There were patches of fertile land around the main settlements, but along the coast the soil was mainly either too sandy or riddled with rock. Local inhabitants grew grain on a small scale, as well as vegetables and sugar cane. They also reared pigs, chickens, goats and cattle. Until the end of the 18th century, mahogany trees grew in abundance, but they were being cut down at such a massive rate, that they were fast dying out.

The population of Cayman in the 18th century consisted of British navy mariners, shipwrecked passengers along with early settlers from Jamaica and Britain and their slaves. It was the plentiful supply of mahogany that attracted these first settlers. By 1700 loggers and planters had arrived to start a new life and plunder the reddish brown timber that covered large patches of the island. Before that time, the settlers and their slaves farmed

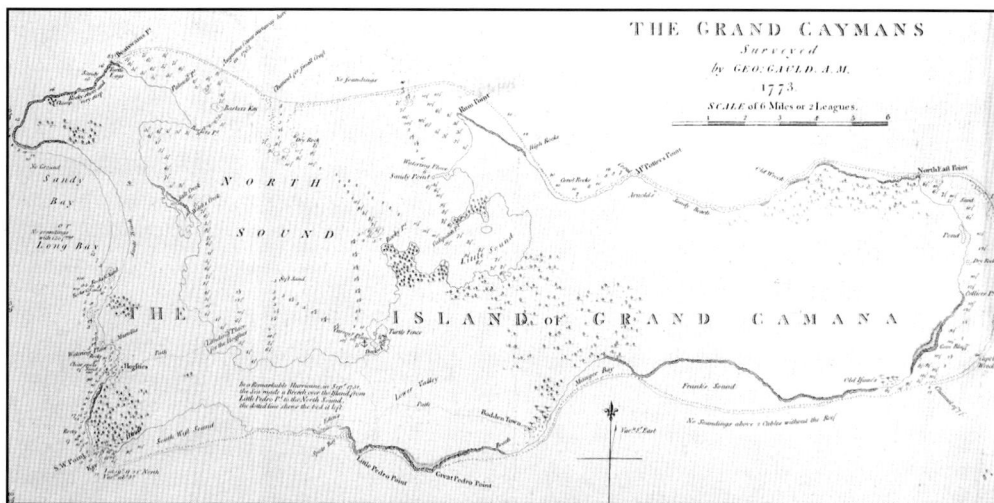

Grand Caymans map 1773: George Gauld
© Crown copyright National Archives

the land with subsistence crops, and fished the warm waters for turtles. When, eventually, the mahogany ran out its place was taken by a new crop – cotton. By the end of the 18th century the population had doubled and when Edward Corbett drew up the first official census at the request of Governor Nugent of Jamaica in 1802, he described the make up of the population as '309 whites, 73 free people of colour, six free negroes and 545 slaves'.

There were no real roads on Grand Cayman at that time, in some cases not even tracks. Rocky paths separated the two main settlements of Bodden Town and George Town or Hogstyes. George Town had a sheltered harbour, deep enough for ships to anchor. The majority of the buildings there were sturdily constructed of wattle and daub. This was a busy port with a fish market, which exists to this day. There was a small fort called Fort George armed with four cannons but by no means well equipped.

Writing his report in the 1802 census Corbett rather dismissively describes the town: 'Georgetown would be most accessible to an enemy, as being the only place where vessels of burden could anchor with security'. At the time, only eighty people on the island were allowed or able to bear arms.

Turtles

One of the main sources of food for islanders and passing ships was turtle meat. The clear warm waters surrounding Grand Cayman were home to large numbers of green sea turtles.

Full of taste, with the density of pork, turtle meat was a favourite food source for passing vessels carrying British Navy mariners, their French enemies or pirates. It was often enthusiastically described as 'the most wholesomest and best provision in all the Indies'.

Turtling had been the mainstay of the islands' exports. Turtles were either carried alive on board or salted to be preserved for long voyages. They were one of the main exports but by the time of the 'Wreck of The Ten Sail' the effect of over fishing was beginning to show and this once thriving industry was fading.

A mature wild Green or Loggerhead turtle can weigh 300 to 400 lbs in the wild (farmed Green turtles can weigh up to 500lbs).

Slavery

Slavery existed in Cayman into the 19th century, but there are opposing views on how harsh slaves' lives actually were. On the one hand historians believe that because there were no large plantations in Cayman, slaves were not exposed to the severe conditions of neighbouring Caribbean islands or America. Others argue that the slave system here was equally oppressive and insist it is irrelevant what form of actual labour was undertaken. As is the case in many societies, the social integration following the end of slavery resulted in a mixed population, which is reflected through subsequent generations. Some historians believe that because the Cayman Islands were very under populated at the time of emancipation, there was enough land for former slaves to establish their own freeholds and thus become part of the growth, expansion and ultimate success of the island.

Mosquitoes

As soon as it became dusk, the survivors of the 'Wreck of the Ten Sail' would have had to face one the most unpleasant aspects of life on Grand Cayman and one that remained a serious problem up until the late 1960s: the swarms of mosquitoes, breeding in their millions in the inland swamps, circling, with ominous high pitched buzzing, getting into ears, eyes, noses and mouths. Feeding from dusk and then often well into the night, the mosquitoes would sometimes offer a few hours respite, before swarming again at dawn. It was generally regarded as foolhardy to venture outside after sunset, although people's houses would not necessarily offer the best protection. During the rainy season, the mosquitoes were even more prevalent. Livestock would be under constant threat because out in the open, mosquitoes could fly in a swarm of millions, entering the noses and mouths of cattle and suffocating them. Smoke-pots were used to keep the mosquitoes at bay, but not always with great success.

Capture

The British West Indies colonies were an important and valuable source of commodities to Britain in the latter half of the 18th century, the more so following the American War of Independence. Jamaica in particular was of strategic importance as well as being a key trading post in the triangular slave trade, whereby merchant ships would trade goods for slaves in West Africa who would be shipped across the Atlantic for sale to the sugar plantation owners. Rich cargoes of sugar, rum, molasses and timber would then be brought back to Britain.

Little more than a week following the execution of Louis XVI and most of his family in Paris on 21st January 1793, the newly declared France Republic declared war on Britain, prompting the Royal Navy to launch an expedition from Jamaica to seize St. Domingue (Haiti).

There was immediate concern for the safety of British merchant shipping sailing from the Caribbean and the Navy was urged to ensure that convoys were afforded adequate protection. One of the first actions against the French in the Caribbean occurred in late 1793. Commodore John Ford, in command of the fleet in the West Indies, took advantage of the Haitian revolution

ADMIRALTY-OFFICE, FEB. 11, 1794.

On Sunday the 9th inftant a letter was received from Commodore Ford, Commander in Chief of his Majefty's fhips at Jamaica, addreffed to Mr. Stephens, dated the 7th of December, 1793, of which the following is an extract, with a copy of the letter to which it refers.

"I requeft you will be pleafed to inform the Lords Commiffioners of the Admiralty, that fince my letter of the 24th of November laft, by the Antelope packet, nothing material has happened to the fquadron under my command, except the capture of the Inconftant French frigate, by the Penelope and Iphigenia, the particulars whereof are ftated in Capt. Rowley's letter to me herein inclofed; and to which I fhall add, (in juftice to the commendable zeal, activity, and enterprize of thofe officers on all occafions, the high condition and difcipline of their fhips) that, in my opinion, either of them alone would have accomplifhed what fell to their united efforts."

Penelope, Port Royal Harbour, Jamaica,
November 30, 1793.

SIR,

I beg leave to acquaint you, that I failed from Mole St. Nicholas on the 20th inftant, having received intelligence that the Inconftant frigate was expected to leave Port au Prince, to convoy a large armed merchantman. On the day following I fell in with his Majefty's fhip Iphigenia, Captain Sinclair, to whom I gave orders to keep company, and was proceeding to Port au Prince, when I was informed from Leoganne that the Inconftant had failed with two fmall veffels for Petit Trou, but was daily expected back.

I immediately made fail, with intention of trying to take or deftroy her in the harbour; but, on the night of the 25th, we had the good fortune to fall in with her, and, after exchanging a few broadfides, fhe ftruck her colours to the frigates.

The Penelope had one man killed and feven wounded; amongft the latter is Mr. John Allen, midfhipman. The Inconftant had fix killed, amongft whom was the Firft Lieutenant; and the Captain and 20 wounded, three of whom are fince dead.

From the gallant behaviour of Lieut. Malcolm, the officers, and fhip's Company, I have every reafon to flatter myfelf, that, had either of his Majefty's frigates been fingle, they would have been equally fortunate in capturing her.

I beg leave to add, that Captain Sinclair's very favourable report of the conduct of his Officers and fhip's company is fuch as does them the greateft honour.   I remain, Sir,

Your moft obedient humble fervant,

B. S. ROWLEY.

John Ford, Efq. Commodore and
Commander in Chief, &c. &c. &c.

Times *12th February 1794*

to occupy several ports in the French colony of Saint-Domingue (now Haiti). On 20 November 1793 HMS *Penelope* sailed from Môle-Saint-Nicolas, having received news that the French 36-gun frigate *L'Inconstante* was sailing from Port-au-Prince, escorting a large merchant ship. The next day HMS *Penelope* met the 32-gun frigate HMS *Iphigenia* and the two ships proceeded towards Port-au-Prince. However they learned that *L'Inconstante* had sailed to Petit Trou with two mail ships, but was soon expected to return to port. They intended to cut her out of the harbour of Port-au-Prince, but on the night of the 25 November met her at sea, and after a brisk exchange of broadsides, *L'Inconstante* surrendered. The *Penelope* had only one man killed and seven wounded, while the *L'Inconstante* had nine killed, including the Captain and the First Lieutenant, and 17 wounded.

Taken as a prize to Port Royal, Jamaica, the *L'Inconstante* was immediately taken into service by the Navy and renamed HMS *Convert*.

By John Ford Esq.r Commodore,
and Commander in Chief
&c. &c. &c.

Whereas the Principal Merchants
and Planters of Jamaica have applied to
me by means of Governor Williamson, for
a Convoy to be appointed to Sail with the
homeward bound Trade about the middle
of this Month.

You are therefore hereby required
and directed to be at Bluefields Bay on
that Island with His Majesty's Ship under
your Command by the 18.th instant, taking
such Merchant Ships as may be ready to
Sail from the Port of Kingston with you,
and having received under your Protection
such Ships as may be assembled at Bluefields,
to put to Sea with them and His Majesty's
Ship under your Command on the 20.th inst.
proceeding (through the Gulf of Florida.)
that Clear in Ireland, if the wind &

Captain Lawford's orders to escort the Jamaica convoy
© Crown copyright National Archives

20

The Convoy

In February 1794, a convoy of 58 merchant ships, escorted by the British naval frigate HMS *Convert,* commanded by 37-year-old Captain John Lawford, set sail from Jamaica for Britain and America. Lawford had arrived in the West Indies in 1790 and promoted to post-captain on the outbreak of war with France in 1793.

The 36-gun *Convert* had previously been a French ship, the *L'Inconstante,* captured by the British the previous year, condemned as a prize of war and renamed. Fifth-rate frigates like the *Convert* were thought to be too light for a major sea battle and so were often relegated to merchant convoy escorts.

Lawford's orders were to steer a course to leeward with the convoy through the Yucatan Channel, passing to the west of Cuba, before heading east through the Florida Straits and following the Gulf Stream across the Atlantic to Britain. The *Convert* set sail from Port Royal on the east side of Jamaica on the 28th January for Bluefields Bay on the other side of the island where she was joined by a fleet of 32 merchantmen. A week later, they sailed west to Long Bay where they were joined by a further 26

vessels from Jamaica's northern ports. The convoy now comprised a total of 58 ships under the protection of the *Convert*, all but three of which were bound for Europe. Most of which were heavily laden with cargoes of sugar, rum, molasses, cotton, timber and other goods.

Such an unwieldy fleet set out with a strong easterly breeze at dawn on Thursday, 6th February, intending to pass well south of the Cayman Islands by the following day. Sailing at the head of the convoy, Captain Lawford had issued instructions and signals to the captains of each merchant ship, including directions designed to keep the convoy together and to keep astern of the *Convert*, mindful of his own orders to 'accommodate your progress to that of the worst sailing ship among them'. The *Convert* herself shortened sail as did the faster ships to ensure they did not outrun the slower vessels.

With a good following breeze, a ship would have expected to pass Grand Cayman within 24 hours of leaving Jamaica. Inevitably perhaps, with such a large flotilla, things did not go quite according to plan. Shortly after dawn the next morning of Friday, 7th February, a schooner among them, one of three bound for North America, fired a gun as a distress signal, having sprung a leak, and the whole convoy had to heave to for several hours while it was attended to and able to continue.

At noon the *Convert*'s sailing master, Thomas Popplewell, accompanied by the Master's Mate and two midshipmen, took bearings with the aid of sextants and quadrants that recorded their position to be on latitude 18° 47' north, a point roughly halfway between Jamaica and Grand Cayman. Popplewell, who had navigated the westerly route from Jamaica through the Florida Straits on several previous occasions, estimated that Grand Cayman lay just over 60 miles to the north-west and marked the position on the ship's chart accordingly.

Navigation

It is unlikely the *Convert* carried a chronometer (which would have enabled longitude to be calculated) so navigation relied on regular observations using a sextant or quadrant. This would be combined with the ship's speed through the water, being calculated by means of the ship's log (dropped overboard and the knots in the log-line counted off over a fixed period of time).

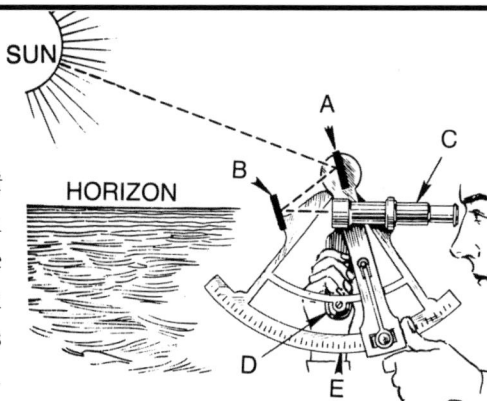

Observations were usually done at four hour intervals, coinciding with the change of watch, and always at noon when the sun was at its zenith. By noting the angle of the sun in relation to the horizon, allowing for the ship's speed through the water and the direction of travel from the compass bearing, it was possible to calculate the ship's latitude and thus, by a method of dead-reckoning, its position on the chart from the previously recorded position – known as 'pricking off'. Such a method could not, of course, take account of the effect of the wind or any currents.

Thomas Popplewell's noon observation aboard the *Convert* on 7th February 1794 as the convoy lay roughly halfway between Jamaica and Grand Cayman, was taken with his sextant. He was accompanied by the Master's Mate, James Hutchins, and two Midshipmen, Colin Campbell and Thomas Sherwin.

An hour later, with the schooner apparently made seaworthy, the convoy was under way again. Aboard the *Convert* however the delay had made Lawford anxious to sight the island of Grand Cayman before dark, normally used as a landmark along the shipping route towards the Yucatan Channel to the east of Mexico. Under foresail and topsails, the *Convert* soon pulled ahead of the rest of the fleet which was making steady progress on a west-north-westerly course.

At around three o'clock in the afternoon, however, the same schooner that had been in trouble earlier fired a gun again and Captain Lawford, aware that several of the vessels in his charge were in poor condition, gave the order to wear ship, heading back into the merchantmen astern of the *Convert*. This time, it emerged that the troublesome schooner had fired a cannon because it feared being left behind by the rest of the convoy.

After yet another delay, the convoy moved off again but by this time Lawford was aware that they would be unlikely to sight Grand Cayman before nightfall. He proceeded cautiously but steadily in a westerly direction throughout the evening, with the frigate's swivel guns occasionally being fired whenever other vessels were running ahead of them.

Popplewell took over as officer of the watch on the quarterdeck from midnight, confident they had gained about 35 miles, leaving them some 25 miles south of Grand Cayman. He advised Lawford that, as the wind had backed round to the north, they should steer a more northerly course in order to round Cape Corientes on the western tip of Cuba. Both men believed they were then well clear of the Cayman Islands.

With the *Convert*'s sails furled and braced aback to slow her through the darkness to keep pace with the slower vessels following together astern, Lawford retired below for the night, leaving Popplewell in charge on the quarterdeck. But sometime after midnight the *Convert* was again overtaken by several merchantmen, apparently unnoticed by the frigate's watch.

At around three o'clock, a ship's gun was heard to fire leeward of the *Convert*. Popplewell went below to inform Lawford who, assuming the shot was a distress signal, gave the order for the *Convert* to make sail and head towards the vessel concerned so that immediate assistance could be provided. But as soon as he reached the quarterdeck he realised that the ship firing the gun was ahead of the *Convert* as indeed were several others. Moments later, a cry was heard from the frigate's topsail yard: "Land and breakers ahead, close to us!"

Immediately the lookout's warning cry was heard by the men on deck aboard the *Convert*. Captain Lawford, realising the peril lurking nearby, ordered a gun to be fired as a signal for the whole convoy to take evasive action and disperse. As the *Convert* itself began to do likewise, the menacing sight of phosphorescence in the sea on all sides in the darkness became apparent; a sure

sign that they were almost upon a reef. But just as the
Convert's superior sailing ability began to steer away from
the danger, one of the merchant vessels on the opposite
tack ahead came crashing into her bow, carrying away
her jib boom. With bowsprit and rigging entangled, the

two vessels remained locked together while the *Convert*'s crew strove to free the frigate; they succeeded briefly only for the same merchant ship to collide with her yet again. By this time, the *Convert* had drifted nearer the breakers and it was apparent they were almost on a reef. Even as her crew managed to disentangle her yet again, nothing could save her. Amid the increasing roar of the surf, the frigate struck the reef. As the sails were being furled, the ship's carpenter reported that the bilge was holed and water had reached the orlop deck.

The Wreck

At daybreak on Saturday, 8th February, the true scale of the disaster was gradually revealed. HMS *Convert* was aground on the coral reef that extended around the eastern end of Grand Cayman less than a mile offshore. Not only was the Convert stuck fast and bilged, but nine other merchant vessels had similarly come to grief on the same reef. Wrecked alongside the *Convert* were the merchant ships *Britannia, Nancy, Ludlow, Moorhall, Richard* and the *William & Elizabeth* as well as the brigs *Sally, Eagle* and *Fortune*.

To make matters worse, a heavy sea was running with a strong southerly onshore wind, preventing any of the surviving 48 convoy ships from approaching close enough to provide assistance. The rough conditions also made it impossible for any small craft ashore to cross the reef and come to the rescue.

Captain Lawford immediately ordered that the *Convert*'s boats be launched, eventually enabling the women passengers, invalid soldiers and other supernumerary members of the ship's company to be taken to the safety of the surviving vessels standing offshore; a difficult and

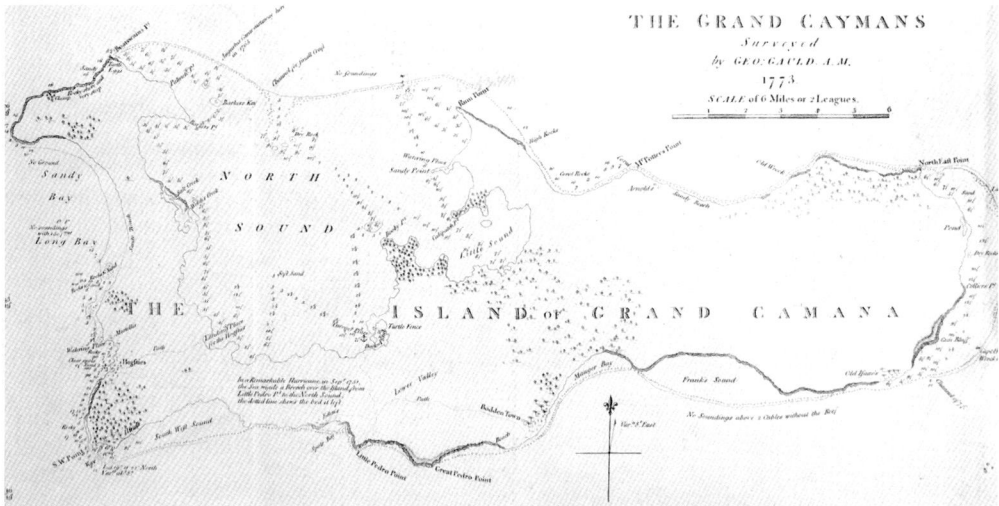

dangerous process in the conditions that took almost all day. Among those transferred to the ships standing offshore were Lieutenant Colonel Jeffrey Amherst of the 10th Regiment of Foot and Lady Amelia Cooke, daughter of the 3rd Duke of Atholl, who were taken aboard the *Louisa*.

The crew meanwhile was employed removing the three masts and other rigging and generally salvaging whatever they could. In the panic and confusion of the night's shipwreck and the ensuing attempts to launch the boats, several men were drowned including the captain of the *Britannia*, Daniel Martin. Some succeeded in swimming through the reef to reach the comparative safety of the lagoon within where they were rescued by canoes manned by the islanders; others managed by launching makeshift rafts. At one point, the *Convert*'s hull shifted on the jagged coral so that it became half submerged as the waves crashed over her.

Throughout the day, as the weather moderated, some semblance of calm and order was gradually restored. By late afternoon, with only a skeleton crew remaining aboard, Captain Lawford decided to set off in the ship's barge with the intention of heading for the west end of Grand Cayman, rowed by ten sailors. Lawford was accompanied by Captain Henry Thompson of the 2nd Battalion, Royal Artillery; the purser, John Scott; Thompson's servant and a French prisoner. Once launched, the barge attempted to round the stern of the *Convert* and head out to sea only to get caught up in the masts and rigging floating alongside. Within minutes, the boat was swamped by a succession of waves and swept in towards certain catastrophe on the reef when a sudden surge somehow carried barge and occupants through the heavy swell and into the calm of the lagoon within.

By nightfall all but Thomas Popplewell and about twenty crewmen chose to remain on board, the rest having either transferred to one of the waiting merchant ships or had managed to get ashore.

SHIP NEWS.

Several Danish vessels, laden with wheat, bound to France, have been carried into Dover.

LIVERPOOL, MARCH 17.

The *Cyclops*, FAIRWEATHER, and *Betsey*, KENT, part of the Jamaica fleet, which sailed under convoy of the *Convert* frigate, arrived here this morning, by whom we learn, that the vessels lost are—the *William* and *Elizabeth*, GOODRICK and LUDLOW, of London; *Eagle*, of Kingston; *Richard*, of Belfast; *Moor Hall*, of Liverpool (people saved); *Britannia* and *Nancy*, of Glasgow, both for London; and two Brigs, names not known, the people not being come on shore; the *Gascoyne*, *Alice*, and *Lord Rodney*, left the Hogsties the day before; the *Betsey* spoke the *Thomas*, HENRY, of Cork, for London, belonging to the fleet, the 2d of March, in lat. 40. 42. long. 51. 0. The fleet, about 70 sail, left Bluefields the 5th of February.

The following letter was sent to the Commanders of the different merchant vessels, by the Captain of the *Convert*:

"GENTLEMEN, *Grand Camaynen, 7th or 8th Feb. 1794.*
"I beg to acquaint you, that the officers and crew of the CONVERT frigate, and merchant vessels, lately wrecked on the reef to the Eastward of this Island, are in the greatest distress, not being able (from the very great surf), to save any provision, or any other necessary convenience—I must therefore desire of you to anchor at the Hogsties, or lay off and on, to take the people on board, as soon as it is possible to get them over: it is impossible to embark them at this part of the island, while the sea is so great."

Times *20th March 1794*

Ashore

The shoreline along the eastern end of Grand Cayman at dawn on Sunday, 9th February, resembled the aftermath of a storm. Beaches littered with flotsam and jetsam; weary and bewildered survivors, some lying on the sand, others wandering among the washed-up remains of the wrecks impaled on the reef out to sea.

The Cayman islanders on that part of the island, still reeling from the devastation of the hurricane that had swept through less than four months earlier destroying almost everything in its path, awoke to the astonishing spectacle of ten ships wrecked offshore. Any thoughts of salvage opportunity were soon dispelled by the realisation that such a multitude of survivors would prove an impossible burden on the island's meagre resources.

Their despair, however, was as nothing compared to that of those that had managed to make it ashore, exhausted and soaked to the skin. It soon became apparent that they were stranded on a desolate island where the miserable conditions of the few local inhabitants they encountered were scarcely better than their own; virtually no food or water to be had, no prospect of dry clothing or bedding either.

Makeshift shelters and tents of sailcloth gradually began to appear along the shoreline as those who had survived the perilous crossing of the reef began to take stock of their parlous situation. Beyond the reef, the sea was at first too rough for the party still aboard the *Convert* to attempt to make it ashore, but by late afternoon a raft had been constructed and launched which enabled some stores and baggage to be brought on land along with the remaining crew members.

Captain Lawford meanwhile wasted no time in penning an urgent message, addressed to the 'Commanders of the Merchant Ships and Vessels off the Island of Grand Cayman' and headed:

> *East end of the Isld of Grand Cayman 9th Feby 1794*
>
> *I beg to acquaint you that the officers and crew of the Convert and the merchant vessels lately wrecked on the reefs to the eastward of this island are in the greatest distress, not being able from the very great surf to save any provisions or any other necessary convenience. I must therefore desire of you, either to anchor at the Hogsties, or lay off and on there ready to take to the people on board as soon as it is possible to get them over, it being impracticable to embark them from this part of the island whilst the sea is so great.*

Lawford's letter to the captains of the merchant vessels
© *Crown copyright National Archives*

The spidery handwriting on one half of a pale blue sheet of notepaper seems to reflect the considerable anxiety and concern Lawford felt at the time as he realised their only hope of escape and rescue was to somehow make their way to the settlement at George Town, otherwise known as the Hogsties, on the west of the island. The letter was taken out to the vessels standing offshore in one of the island's canoes.

His despair at the enormity of the disaster that had befallen his ship and the men he commanded was shared by everyone, almost all of whom had lost personal possessions and were ill-equipped to survive in the open under the glare of the sun. What few items such as clothing, books and papers they had managed to salvage were mostly ruined.

By Monday, the following day, the weather had moderated sufficiently to allow some of the *Convert*'s men to return to the hulk beyond the reef and salvage as much of the ship's stores as they could manage. Sails, hammocks, buckets, several casks of salt beef as well as timber, spars and other equipment from the carpenter's stores were brought ashore, but much of the provisions and equipment on board could not be recovered. Two barrels of rum were fortuitously rescued but all the ship's bread was ruined by seawater.

On Tuesday morning, Captain Lawford set off on foot, heading west across the island, accompanied by Captain Henry Thompson of the 2nd Battalion, Royal Artillery, a local guide and another army officer. The eighteen mile journey over scorching sand, sharp jagged coral rocks under a blazing sun would have taxed the fittest men, let alone those already weakened by shipwreck, thirst and hunger. Captain Thompson, himself a seasoned army officer, was later to describe their ordeal as being 'over the most execrable road imaginable … that would have foiled the attempts of the most dexterous animal to pass without injury'.

The party of four men would have passed through Bodden Town, the island's main settlement, though the inhabitants there, still recovering from the hurricane that had devastated the island in October 1793, were in no position to offer assistance. When they arrived eventually at George Town at noon the following day they found nine of the convoy's surviving merchantmen had heeded Lawford's request and were already at anchor there.

News of the catastrophe in Gun Bay at the other end of Grand Cayman had already reached the inhabitants of George Town. The sudden arrival of the three hundred surviving crew and passengers of the *Convert* as well as those from the other wrecked merchantmen scattered along the shore in the aftermath of the devastation caused by the hurricane raised the prospect of an immediate humanitarian crisis for everyone on the island. Lawford was soon confronted with a petition from eight leading islanders demanding the immediate removal of their unwanted visitors as soon as possible:

Geo: Town 12th Feby 1794

Capt. John Lawford Sir

We the Subscribers, Inhabitants of
of the Island Grand Camanus do Certify on oath
that from the distress & Situation of the Island
in the Article of Provisions, owing to the
Hurricane of the 19th Octr last, It's morally
impossible for the Inhabitants to support
themselves, And with the Addition of the
different Ships Companies wrecked on
the East End of this Island on Saturday
Morning last, We the Subscribers think
it absolutely necessary for own preservation
that the different Crews belonging to the Wrecks
already specified, must be immediately removed
from this Island as soon as possible We
are with the utmost respect Sir
Your most obedt Servts

turn over

We the Subscribers, Inhabitants of the Island Grand Camanas do certify on oath that from the distressed situation of the Island, in the article of provisions, owing to the Hurricane of the 19th Octr. last. Its morally impossible for the inhabitants to support themselves, and with the addition of the different Ships Companies wrecking on the East End of this Island on Saturday morning last.

We the Subscribers think it absolutely necessary for own preservation, that the difft crews belonging to the wrecks already specified must be immediately removed from this Island as soon as possible.

The seven signatories included George Turnbull, who also signed on behalf of William Bodden, the island's Chief Magistrate; Joseph Dalby, Robert Knowles Clarke, Thomas Thomson, William Great Prescott, Hugh Mitchell and James Hoy.

The islanders had been receiving some relief aid in the weeks following the hurricane, mostly provided by merchant vessels carrying urgently needed provisions from Jamaica. But it was scarcely sufficient for the population of around 700 inhabitants at the time, some two-thirds of whom were slaves, let alone double that number. Their concern was shared by Lawford who wrote another letter to the captains of the nine merchant ships anchored offshore, pleading with them to take as many of the shipwrecked crews as possible:

George Town Grand Cayman
13th Febry. 1794

Gentlemen

        The Inhabitants of this
Island have represented to me that from
the distressed situation in the article of
Provisions owing to the Hurricane of the
19th of October last, It is morally impos=
=sible for them to support themselves,
with the addition of the different Ships
Crews Wrecked on the East end of this
Island on Saturday morning, and beg
that they may be removed immediatly,
which on the Strictest investigation
I find to be a just report. I have
therefore to desire that you will
receive as many of the above mentioned
Seamen on board the Ships & Vessels you
respectively Command. as You can
Possibly accommodate, and on your
arrival in England deliever them to
the Commanding officer on the Impress
Service at any of the Ports, or onboard
any of His Majestys Ships, you may

fall in with, sending regular lists
and taking receipts, at the same time
transmitting an account to the Lords
Commissioners of the Admiralty of the
expences of Victualling &c, during
there Passage I am
                    Gentlemen
        Your most obedient
            humble Servant
                J. Lawford

To Captains Bryan — Ship Alfred
        „ Harrison — — — Louisa
        „ Adams — — — Landovery
        „ Gamble — — „Jane„
        „ Moore — — Barbadoe
        „ Campbell — Nancy
        „ Harvey — Brig Betsey & Susan
        „ Ogden — — Do. Countess of Galloway
        „ King — Do. Mail —

Copy
Jn. Lawford

Lawford's letter to the captains of the nine merchant vessels
anchored in Hog Sty Bay, 13th February 1794

© Crown copyright National Archives

41

The Inhabitants of this Island have represented to me that, from the distressed situation in the Article of Provisions owing to the Hurricane of 19th Octr last, it is morally impossible for them to support themselves with the addition of the different Ships Crews wrecked on the East End of the Island on Saturday Morning, and I beg that they may be removed immediately; which on the strictest investigation I find to be a just Report: I have therefore to desire that you will receive as many of the above mentioned Seamen on board the vessels you respectively command as you can possibly accommodate; and on your arrival in England deliver them to the Commanding Officer on the Impress Service at any of the Ports or on board of any of His Majesty's Ships of War that you may fall in with, sending regular lists & taking receipts; and transmitting at the same time to the Lords Commissioners of the Admiralty an Account of the Expenses of Victualling &c. during the passage.

The letter, dated 13th February, was addressed to the captains of the nine merchantmen and copies were delivered to Brenton Bryan of the *Alfred*; Thomas Harrison of the *Louisa*; William Adams of the *Llandovery*; Captain Gammell of the *Jane*; Captain Moore of the *Barbados*; Robert Campbell of the *Nancy*; Captain Harvey of the *Betsey & Susan*; William Elgin of the *Countess of Galloway* and Captain King of the *Mars*.

The captains were also given copies of a letter written by Lawford addressed to the 'Governor of Havannah' on Cuba, requesting that the ships and their occupants be provided with whatever assistance they needed.

Captain Thompson, the army officer who had accompanied Lawford on the arduous trek across the island, boarded the *Louisa* where he joined Colonel Jeffrey Amherst and Lady Amelia Cooke among the other passengers rescued from the *Convert* including Lieutenent Brice, an officer from HMS *Hermione* invalided home, who was entrusted with Lawford's official report to the Admiralty concerning the loss of the *Convert*. On Friday, 13th February, they weighed anchor and set sail for Cuba.

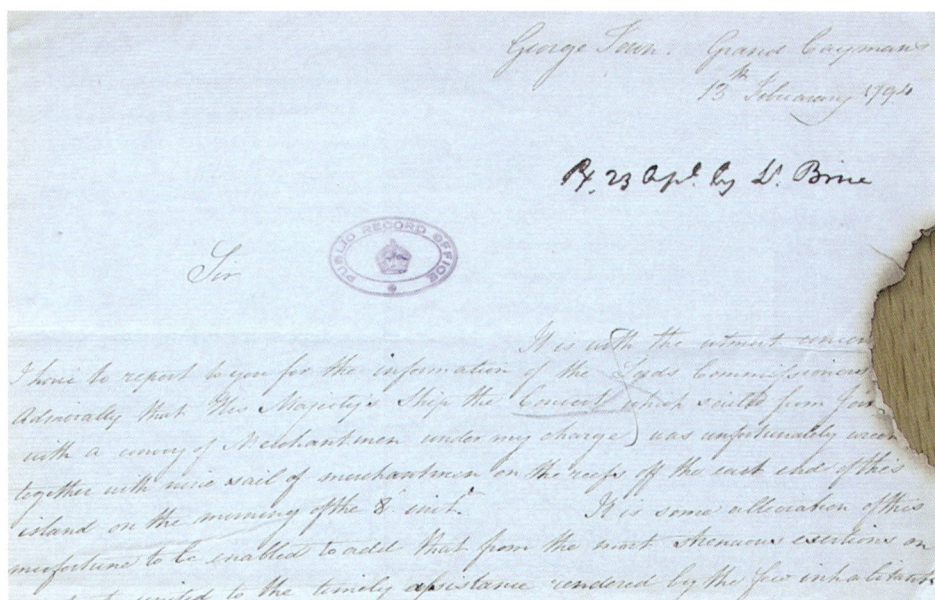

Lawford's report to the Admiralty, 13th February 1794, entrusted to Lieutenant Brice, a survivor of the wreck of HMS Convert

© Crown copyright National Archives

The JAMAICA CONVOY.

We are extremely forry to confirm the news we gave in our paper of yesterday, concerning the fate of part of this fleet. The news was so little known that it was not believed either at Lloyd's, or the Jamaica Coffee-house, in the early part of the morning. The following is the letter which has been officially received on the subject; and we trust that such a naval force will be instantly sent to sea to protect the arrival of this valuable fleet, which is now coming home with a convoy of only an 18 gun ship, as will secure, as far as it is possible, its safe arrival in the ports of Great Britain.

Extract of a Letter from Capt. THOMPSON, *of the Diana merchant ship, arrived in the Downs, from Jamaica, to his owners.* DOWNS, *March* 17.

"I arrived here in 36 days from Jamaica. I left the island the 6th Feb. under convoy of the Convert frigate, with about 50 sail.

"I am forry to add, that my time under her protection was of short duration; as the frigate, with nine sail of the convoy, was unfortunately wrecked between twelve and one o'clock on the morning of the 8th. At daylight I was a spectator of their total destruction on a reef of rocks, that lies at the east end of the Grand Carmanoes. The fleet stood off and on until three in the afternoon, endeavouring to get the people off, but I, having no boats, could give no affistance, and immediately fet fail. I cannot give you the names of any but the Sally, of Kingston.

Times *18th March 1794*

44

Salvage

Having arranged for most of the surviving members of his crew to be transferred to the merchant ships that continued on to Havana, Captain Lawford returned to Gun Bay where the *Convert*'s officers and about thirty chosen crew members were engaged in the task of salvaging whatever they could from the wreck on the reef. Their temporary accommodation on the shore consisted of makeshift huts and tents using whatever sailcloth they had managed to rescue.

Lawford passed some of the time writing a lengthy report to Commodore John Ford, relating the circumstances leading up to the loss of the *Convert* and the other nine ships in the convoy. The account ran to nearly a dozen pages and reveals the desperate state that he and his men were in at the time:

> *The peculiar and embarrassed situation in which I am now, having lost almost everything and without the smallest convenience... We are at present hutted and under tents in the best manner possible opposite the wreck which is about two miles from the shore, and from our unfavourable situation, very few*

Island of Grand Cayman
Febry 20th, 1794

Sir

It is with extreme concern
that I have to report to you that His
Majesty's Ship Convert was unfortunately
wrecked, together with nine Sail of Mer=
=chant Men under my convoy on the Reefs
off the East end of the Grand Cayman on the
morning of the 8th instant, but it is some
alleviation of this Misfortune to be
enabled to add, that from the most
strenuous exertions on our parts, and the
timely Assistance rendered by the few
Inhabitants (by all the Means in their
power) few lives were lost.

I had the honor to write you
from Bluefields Bay on the 3d instant,
informing you of my Intention of Sailing
with the Ships that had rendezvoused
there, on that day, but light westerly
winds and a calms prevailing rendered it
impossible for the heavy Merchant Vessels
to quit the Bay before the morning of the
5th, when I got under weigh at daylight
with about thirty two Sail, & brought

Lawford's report from Gun Bay to Commodore John Ford
© Crown copyright National Archives

46

articles has been practicable to get on shore, except two puncheons of rum and some few casks of provisions, the bread is totally spoiled and the miserable situation of this Island precludes us from being furnished with anything of the bread kind.

He concluded with an evidently heartfelt expression of the wretchedness of his situation:

Truly convinced of the Magnitude of this Calamity and Knowing its evil influence on the Commerce of my Country in whose service I have pass'd my Life; my Distress of mind would be unsupportable were I not supported by a Consciousness of having done my Duty.

The *Convert's* First Lieutenant, Joseph Bradby Bogue, was entrusted with the task of delivering Lawford's report to Commodore Ford. As soon as news of the disaster reached Port Royal in Jamaica, several merchant ships set sail for the Cayman Islands. Ford meanwhile was at sea aboard his flagship, HMS *Europa* and did not learn of the loss of the Convert and the other convoy vessels until five weeks after the event. He immediately sent the 32-gun frigate HMS *Success,* commanded by Captain Francis Roberts, to Grand Cayman.

By the time the Success arrived off George Town on 17th March, the remaining band of *Convert* survivors had been camped out in make-shift tents along the shore of Gun

Bay for thirty-six days while attempting to salvage what they could from the wreck out on the reef. Apart from four ship's boats, a few sails, spars, ropes and rigging tackle and several weapons and other items from the gunner's stores, not much else had been brought ashore other than sixteen casks of beef and the remains of a cask of rum. None of the *Convert*'s 12-pounder cannons was recovered before what was left of the wreck sank beneath the waves.

Before Lawford and his men returned to Jamaica aboard the *Success* both he and Captain Roberts arranged with two prominent islanders, William Bodden senior and Robert Knowles Clark, for them to continue salvaging whatever they could from the *Convert*. Both men had been among the eight signatories of the petition demanding the immediate departure of the convoy survivors following the wreck.

> *We the undersigned do hereby bind and oblige ourselves in the most solemn manner to use our utmost endeavour to save all the remaining Stores, Provisions & Guns together with all the Materials of the wreck of His Majesty's Ship Convert such as Iron work, old Copper and Copper fastening, and to give a most faithful & just account if the same.*
>
> *Given under our hands at Grand Caymanas this 19th day of March 1794*

We the undersigned do hereby bind and oblige ourselves in the most solemn manner to use our utmost endeavour to save all the remaining Stores, Provisions, & Guns together with all the Materials of the Wreck of His Majesty's Ship Convert such as Iron Work, old Copper, and Copper fastening, and to give a most faithful & just account of the same.

Given under our hands at Grand Caymanas this 19th day of March 1794

Wm Bodden Senr

Robt Knowles Clarke

(A Copy)

William Bodden senior and Robert Knowles Clark
agreement to continue salvage operations on the wrecks

© Crown copyright National Archives

Meanwhile, whatever stores and equipment that had been salvaged were brought round to the *Success* and loaded aboard her before she set sail again for Jamaica. Following the frigate's arrival at Port Royal at the end of March 1794, Commodore Ford at once ordered a court martial to be held to enquire into the circumstances surrounding the loss of the *Convert* and the nine merchant vessels from the convoy she was escorting.

LLOYD's LIST.

LONDON, FRIDAY MARCH 21, 1794.

THE MARINE LIST.

The Amphitrite Armed Ship has taken and brought into Dover the Margaretha Dorothea, Wallis, from Dort for the Streights.

The Nancy, Campbell, and the Britannia, Martin, of Glasgow; the Eagle, Ainsworth, of Kingston; the Ludlow, M'Lure, and William and Elizabeth, Goodwin, all for London; the Richard, ———, for Belfast; the Moorhall, ———, for Liverpool; and a Brig, were lost on the Grand Camanus; with the Convert Frigate, and Brig Sally of Kingston.

Three Brothers, Rofs	———
Deborah, Williams	Gronengen
———, Storey	Stockholm
Betfey, Halhet	Lifbon
Fame, Hamefley	ditto
Thames Linder	Hambro'
Fame, Cheap	Cadiz
Queen, Harris	ditto
Thyme, ———	ditto
Jupiter, Watkins	Malaga
Minerva, Crawford	Rofs
Diana, Thompfon	Jamaica
Young —, Stonehoufe	Hambro'
Hunter, Blanch	Saloe
Vrow Maddalena, Hooper	Embden
19 Enterprize, Franklin	Cork

An Account of Stores saved from the Wreck of His Majesty's Ship Convert –

Boatswains

Sails	22 N?	Boats Grapnels	2 N?
Pieces of Canvas	3 „	Fire and Chain	1 „
Hammock Covers	4 „	Tackle Hooks	2 „
Compasses	3 „	Travellers	2 „
Stream Cable	1 „	Marline Spikes	2 „
Hawsers	2 „	Anchor Stream	1 „
Messengers	2 „	„ Kedge	1 „
Topsail Sheets	3 „	Time Glasses	6 „
Buoy	1 „	Lengths of Junk	37 „
Leather Buckets	8 „	Boats	4 „
Cat Blocks	2 „	„ Oars	18 „
Coils of Rope	8½ „	„ Masts	6 „
Spare Tackles	8 „	„ Sails	6 „
Blocks of Sorts	125 „	Colours	22 „

Carpenters

		Iron Tiller	1 N?
Topsail Yards	2 N?	Caps	3 „
Lower d?	1 „	Pintles	4 „
Topmasts	3 „	Adzes	2 „
Fish	1 „		1 „

Accounts of the Ships Company that I can at
present collect, and should have sent a List
of the Convoy, had not that, with my other
papers been lost. We are at present hutted
and under Tents in the best manner possible
opposite the wreck which is about two
Miles from the Shore and from our unfortunate
situation very few Articles has been
practicable to get onshore, except two
Puncheons of Rum and some few Casks of
Provisions, the Bread is totally spoiled &
the miserable situation of this Island
precludes us from being furnished with
any thing of the Bread kind.

An extract of Captain Lawford's account to Commodore Ford, 20th February 1794, detailing the circumstances leading up to and following the wreck of HMS Convert

© Crown copyright National Archives

Court Martial

At eight o'clock on the morning on Tuesday, 1st April, a signal was hoisted aboard HMS *Success* at anchor alongside the *Europa, Iphigenia, Goelan* and *Powerful* in Port Royal Harbour, Jamaica. This was swiftly followed by the firing of a single gun to mark the convening of the court-martial that had been ordered to enquire into the loss of the *Convert*.

The court-martial was presided over by Captain Francis Roberts, the commander of the *Success* and the senior naval captain then in Port Royal. He was accompanied by Captain Patrick Sinclair, commander of HMS *Iphigenia;* Captain George Gregory of Ford's 50-gun flagship, HMS *Europa*; Captain William Albany Otway of the 74-gun HMS *Powerful*; and Captain George Henry Stephens of the 14-gun sloop HMS *Goelan*, captured from the French the previous year. The actual running of the court was delegated to the judge advocate, a naval officer named Holmes.

Captain Lawford and six other officers and crew of the *Convert* who had travelled to Jamaica aboard the *Success* from Grand Cayman were brought into the captain's great cabin at the stern of the ship, where the five blue-

Minutes of a Court Martial assembled and held on Board His Majestys Ship Success in Port Royal Harbour Jamaica on the 5th of April 1794

Present
Captain Francis Roberts Commander of His Majestys Ship Success and Senior Captain of His Majestys Ships and Vessels in Port Royal Harbour, President.

Captains

Patrick Sinclair ————— William Albany Otway
George Gregory, George H. Stephens

Captain John Lawford Commander, with such of the Officers & Company of His Majestys late Ship the Convert, as were at Jamaica, were brought into Court, and the Evidence & Audience admitted.

Read the Order of John Ford Esqr Commodore and Commander in Chief of His Majestys Ships & Vessels employed at and about Jamaica &c dated the 30th past, directed to the President to enquire into the Conduct of Captain John Lawford Commander of His Majestys late Ship the Convert, and such of the Officers and Company as were on Board her at the time she was wrecked, together with Nine Sail of Merchant Men, on the Reefs to the Eastward of the Grand Cayman, on the 8th of February last; as she was proceeding to great Britain, agreeably to the Order of the said Commander in Chief, and to Try them for the same Accordingly.

coated judges were assembled. Beyond them, through the panelled windows that formed almost the entire stern wall of the cabin lay Port Royal Harbour.

Commodore Ford's order of 30th March for the court-martial 'to enquire into the conduct of Captain John Lawford, commander of His Majesty's late ship the *Convert,* and such of the officers and company as were on board her at the time she was wrecked, together with nine sail of merchant men, on the reefs to the eastward of the Grand Cayman...' was read. The members of the court then took oaths as directed by the 1749 Naval Act of Parliament.

The judge advocate then read Lawford's letter to his Commander-in-Chief, written on the 20th February on Grand Cayman following the loss of the *Convert,* in which he reported 'with extreme concern' that the *Convert* 'was unfortunately Wreck'd together with Nine Sail of Merchantmen under my Convoy, on the Reefs of the East end of the Grand Cayman on the morning of 8th Instant; but it is some Alleviation of this misfortune to be enabled to add, that from the most Strenuous exertions on our part, and the timely assistance rendered by the Few Inhabitants (by all the means in their power) few Lives were lost'.

Captain Lawford was then asked whether he had any 'charge' to make against any of his officers or men and replied that he had none.

The first of the *Convert*'s officers to be examined was First Lieutenant Joseph Bradby Bogue who described in detail how the convoy had set out from Jamaica on the morning of 6th February, steering west-north-west until evening when they furled the frigate's sails 'not to run too far ahead of the bad sailing vessels'. When he took over as officer of the watch at eight o'clock on the morning of the 7th February the *Convert* was lying-to and her jolly boat alongside the schooner in the convoy that had made a distress signal. Four hours later, with the schooner baled out, the convoy got under way again, only to be delayed again that afternoon by the same schooner signalling that they feared being able to keep up with the rest of the fleet. The convoy continued until nightfall without incident other than the *Convert* firing one of its swivel guns as a warning to some of the convoy ships that were running ahead of their escort.

'At about half past two o'clock on the morning of the 8th, I was awoke and informed there was some firing ahead,' Bogue told the court. 'I immediately went upon deck and found the topsails were loose and sheeting home, which was done and they were hoisted as quick as possible and the helm ordered to be put to port, in order to haul to the northward, but as we were bracing up, the Master from forward called out "a ship ahead almost close to us" when the topsails were braced back, but the ship being on the other tack drove athwart hawse and carried away our jib boom'.

He described how the *Convert* managed to free itself from the other ship that had collided with her, only for the two vessels to crash together a second time. 'Before we could extricate ourselves the ship struck; the master at this time being forward clearing the anchors and sounding. On her striking, the sails were immediately clewed up and furled, top gallant yards got down, and the people were getting the top gallant masts down when the carpenter reported the ship was making water, and in ten minutes after, it was up to the orlop deck, the boats were hoisted out but the ship had by that time bilged and it was found impossible to save the ship: and the lives of the people were preserved with much difficulty except about five who were lost'.

Bogue was then asked by Captain Lawford if the *Convert* had continually signalled to the rest of the vessels in the convoy for those at the rear to make more sail to keep up and for those at the front to shorten sail and not run ahead of their escort. The first lieutenant replied that very little attention was paid to the *Convert*'s signals, adding that it was frequently necessary to keep them in close formation by firing shots with a six pounder cannon mounted on the forecastle.

Bogue's testimony was followed by Second Lieutenant William Earnshaw who, when asked, agreed that some of the vessels in the convoy had been 'very inattentive' to the *Convert*'s signals. He told the court that when he began his watch on deck at eight o'clock on the night of the 7th Captain Lawford had instructed him 'with great anxiety'

Popplewell's testimony was crucial as it had been his knowledge and advice that Lawford would have relied on when agreeing to the fatal course set by his sailing master. When it came to Lawford's turn to question Popplewell, he agreed that if all the convoy vessels had kept to their stations astern of the *Convert* when the breakers were first sighted there would have been time to warn them of the danger and avoid the reef. As for the *Convert* herself, she would have cleared the reef had it not collided with one of the merchant ships. 'Every exertion was used to save the ship and to give the convoy warning to save themselves; many guns were fired and signals made', he added.

Lieutenant Bogue was re-examined by the court concerning the apparent omission of any distance sailed by the *Convert* between noon and four o'clock on the afternoon of the 7th and evidence was heard briefly from the remaining two members of the *Convert*'s crew present, James Hutchins, the Master's Mate, and Midshipman Colin Campbell.

Finally the Master of HMS *Success*, the frigate that had been dispatched to Grand Cayman to assist with salvage operations, was called to give evidence. Richard Davy confirmed that he had encountered a considerable northerly current during the *Success*'s passage from Jamaica to the island, in support of Popplewell's earlier testimony.

Qest.r Do you remember in your passage in the Success
from Jamaica to the Caymans, whether you
found a Northerly Current.

Ans.r We did, a Considerable one.

Qest.r How far Did it set you to the Northward of your
reckoning.

Ans.r I suppose about 9 or 10 Leagues.

(Withdrew)

Here the Examination closed: the Court was clear-
-ed and the Members having maturely weigh'd &
Considered every Circumstance attending the loss be-
-fore mentioned; were of opinion, that it was occasi-
-oned by a strong Current setting the Ship very
considerably to the Northward of the reckoning; &
therefore adjudged that the said Captain John
Lawford Commander of His Majesty's late Ship
the Convert, and such of the Officers and Company
as were on Board her at the time she was wreckd
together with nine Sail of Merchantmen, on the
Reef to the Eastward of the Grand Cayman on
the Morning of the 8.th of February last should be
acquitted. The Court was opened, Audience admit-
-ted, and sentence passed accordingly.

R. Holmes Offg Judge Advocate

© Crown copyright National Archives

61

The court was cleared, and the seven post captains remained to deliberate. It would have been an anxious time for Captain Lawford and Thomas Popplewell since the evidence clearly indicated that it had been a navigational error that had resulted in the loss of the *Convert*. In the event, the verdict of the court, when it came was one of considerable relief to both. The Court, Captain Francis Roberts declared, 'having maturely weighed and considered every circumstance attending the loss … were of the opinion that it was occasioned by a strong current setting the ship very considerably to the northward of the reckoning'.

Captain Lawford and the officers and crew aboard the *Convert* at the time she was wrecked 'together with nine sail of merchantmen on the reefs to the westward of Grand Cayman' were duly acquitted.

Captain John Lawford

Fortunately for John Lawford, the loss of the *Convert* did not adversely affect his naval career. Indeed, he went on to have a long and distinguished one, retiring as a full admiral with a knighthood more than half a century later.

Following his acquittal at the court martial in Jamaica in 1794, Lawford remained in service with the Royal Navy until January 1798 when he was given command of the 64-gun HMS *Agincourt*. Six months later, while in command of the 50-gun HMS *Romney* he intercepted a Swedish convoy in the English Channel; the incident led to strained relations between Britain and Sweden, Denmark and Russia.

In 1800, he was in command of the 64-gun HMS *Polyphemus* when it was part of Rear-Admiral Horatio Nelson's fleet at the Battle of Copenhagen. Another highlight of Lawford's career was the capture of a Spanish frigate returning from South America carrying more than one million dollars in coinage. The seizure resulted in a handsome share of the prize money.

He was promoted to rear-admiral in 1811, a full admiral in 1832 and was made a Knight Commander of the Order of the Bath in 1838 for his gallantry at Copenhagen 37 years previously, the only captain who fought at the battle to receive any honours related to it.

Admiral Sir John Lawford KCB died at his home in St Johns Wood in London three years later at the age of 86, having spent 65 years in service with the Royal Navy spanning the American War of Independence, the French Revolutionary Wars and Napoleonic Wars.

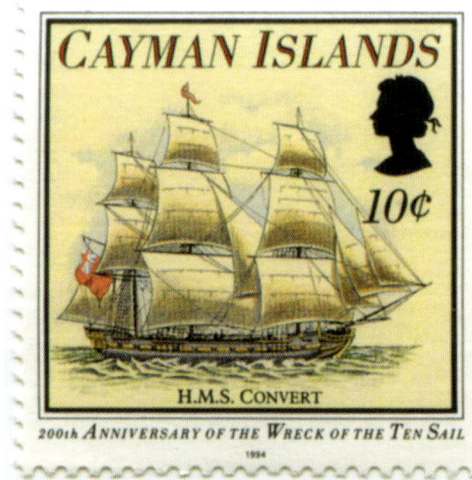

The Legend

There have been many accounts of the wrecking of HMS *Convert* and the nine merchant vessels on Grand Cayman in the years since the maritime disaster in 1794, many of them inaccurate and often exaggerated. But one persistent theme has endured; that among the survivors was a British prince and George III, in gratitude for the islanders' efforts, granted the Cayman Islands its present tax advantageous status.

George III had seven sons who survived into adulthood, two of whom saw active service in the West Indies:

William, Duke of Clarence, who later became King William IV, served in the Royal Navy there under Nelson until 1790. His younger brother Edward, Duke of Kent, was a major-general in the army in the West Indies campaign in 1794.

Since neither are mentioned in the official reports of the loss of HMS *Convert* it is almost certain that they were not aboard the frigate when she ran aground on Grand Cayman in 1794. However new research reveals there were passengers on board who did have close connections with the British monarchy at the time...

Two of the surviving passengers aboard HMS *Convert* when she struck the reef off Grand Cayman had close connections with King George III at the time.

Lieutenant Colonel **Jeffrey Amherst**, an officer in the 10th Regiment of Foot stationed on Jamaica in 1794, was the illegitimate son of Baron Amherst, a former commander-in-chief of the army in North America who was later appointed Governor of Guernsey by King George III. His father, Lord Jeffrey Amherst, was visited by King George III and the Queen at his home Montreal Park in Kent in 1778.

Lady Amelia Cooke was the eldest daughter of the 3rd Duke of Atholl whose aristocratic Murray family ruled the Isle of Man in the 18th century. Thirty-years-old at the time of the wreck, she was returning to England following the death of her husband, Captain Thomas Ivie Cooke, in Jamaica in 1793. He had served as a cavalry officer with the Jamaica Regiment of Light Dragoons.

Her cousin, Lady Augusta Murray (left) had secretly married Prince Augustus Frederick, the sixth son of George III in Italy in April 1793. The prince had been spending time on a grand tour of southern Europe, on the advice of his doctors, to avoid the damp and inclement English weather. Unlike his more robust siblings, Prince Augustus Frederick suffered from extremely poor health, and was severely asthmatic. By 1792 he had reached Rome where he joined a group of English aristocrats living abroad. It was there that he met Lady Augusta Murray, the cousin of the shipwrecked Lady Amelia Cooke (née Murray).

Augustus married Augusta without the consent of his father. The King had passed the Royal Marriages Act in 1772, which forbade any of his descendants to marry without his consent. Any marriage that contravened this act was deemed void, and any offspring would also be illegitimate. On their return to England the couple took their wedding vows once more in secret at St George's in Hanover Square. By this time Augusta was pregnant. Their first child, a boy named Augustus Frederick, was born on January 13th 1794, a few weeks before the Wreck of the Ten Sail.

In 1994, on the 200th anniversary of the calamity, Queen Elizabeth II visited the island's East End and dedicated a memorial to the six victims. On a cliff looking out to the reef where the ships were wrecked, a stone monument  and plaque to commemorate the event were unveiled. Perched along the cliff adjacent to the monument are six small concrete blocks representing the unfortunate few souls the Caymanians were unable to rescue.

King George III

King George III imposed many taxes during his reign at home and also in the British colonies of America. First there was the Sugar Tax of 1764 on the import of molasses, followed by the Stamp Act of 1765 that demanded every legalised document to carry the official government stamp, and finally, and most damaging of all to relations between Britain and America, was the Tea Act of 1773. It was this famous tax that lit the fuse for American Independence and the subsequent loss of the American Colonies in 1776.

During a turbulent reign spanning sixty years, which saw Britain victorious over France in the Seven Years War and the success of the Industrial Revolution, King George was plagued by mental health problems, which perhaps unfairly resulted in his sobriquet the 'Mad King'. Some historians believe that his mental health problems were caused by the condition porphyria.

Cayman Today

Until 1962 the Cayman Islands were a dependency of Jamaica, but when Jamaica voted for independence, the Caymanians decided to maintain their ties with Britain. Today the Cayman Islands are what is known as a British Overseas Territory. The UK appoints a governor every four years and the Premier resides over the local government, with elections taking place every four years. The laws are based on English law, enforced by the Royal Cayman Islands Police Force. Driving is on the left.

Pictures of the Queen and Prince Phillip in the arrival hall at the airport might give the impression of a mini Britain overseas, but this is definitely not the case. With Miami less than 500 miles away, Cayman feels more American that British.

Population

60,000 people live in the Cayman Islands. There are over 135 nationalities living and working side by side. Caymanians make up the biggest group, followed by Jamaican, British, American, Canadian, Filipino, Honduran and other Latin American nationalities. The racial make-up is mixed race 40%, African descent 20 %, European descent 20%, and expatriate of various ethnic groups 20%.

Race relations in Cayman are generally accepted as being extremely good. Caymanians are proud to consider their country as a genuine melting pot with so many different nationalities living and working together.

Cost of Living

This is higher than in the UK, the USA or Canada because practically everything is imported, so the cost of shipping and customs is added on to the price. However it must be remembered that there is no income, inheritance, corporation, sales, capital gains, property or withholding tax.

Tax Free Status

Cayman's status as a leading financial centre can be traced back to the 1960s when pioneers in business and government introduced legislation that sought to maximise the benefits of a tax-free environment. Those early practitioners created a framework that would encourage further economic growth in a jurisdiction without direct taxation on individuals and corporations based on income or wealth.

This formed the impetus to attract more international banks to Cayman as well as law and accounting firms. After the Bahamas became independent from the UK in 1973, expatriate workers from there were attracted to Cayman as a stable place to do business. Today, the working relationship between Government and the private sector remains a co operative one.

Financial Centre

The Cayman Islands have a world class reputation as one of the leading financial centres in the world. It is the world's leading domicile for offshore hedge funds, the second largest captive insurance centre and a leading jurisdiction for banking, trusts, capital markets and fiduciary services.

The islands attract many of the world's top professionals in areas of law, accountancy, corporate services and investment expertise. This coupled with an expanding local workforce of well qualified Caymanians, all helps to boost an already highly successful finance industry.

Law and Order

Crime remains relatively low compared with other Caribbean islands and certainly the rest of the world. A high standard of living is generally enjoyed. But away from the glitzy playground of speed boats, private jets and luxurious beach homes, lies another huge pillar of Cayman life – the Church. This along with a strong sense of civic duty and numerous active charities, plays a significant part in daily life here. Children are encouraged to volunteer and get involved in the community to help elders and those less fortunate. Feed Our Future, Meals on Wheels and the Rotarians are among many organisations offering a helping hand. This is not just an expat activity, in fact some of the most philanthropic are the many wealthy and highly successful Caymanians whose families can be traced back to the founding fathers of the island.

Tourism

The East End of Cayman is the part of the island where the 'Wreck of the Ten Sail' occurred. This is a long way from the bustling finance centre or the cruise ships in George Town. It has a distinctly village feel, and it is easy to step back in time and imagine what it would have been like in the 1700s.

Over on the west side of Grand Cayman, the powdery white sand of Seven Mile Beach (which is actually only 6.3 miles long) has won awards for its breath-taking beauty. The water is pristine; there are no rivers and therefore no run off into the sea. The strip along Seven Mile Beach stretches along the fine white sand with impressive four and five star hotels, condos, restaurants and private beach villas. On the other side of the street are pastel colour plazas lined with boutiques, and restaurants, banks and offices.

People say the real beauty of the Cayman Islands is the water that surrounds them. Water sports are a big part of life for tourists but also for residents enjoying the warmth and year round possibilities of being in the water, be it snorkelling, diving, paddle-boarding, jet-skiing, horseback riding, or kite surfing. Boats are a way of life, either fishing in a small outboard in the early hours of a pink and orange Cayman morning, on a flybridge cruiser or on a pleasure craft heading over to the world famous Stingray City, a sand bar where tourist boats stop, passengers ease themselves into the warm turquoise water and swim with the rays. On Sunday afternoon there is a tradition as important to some as attending church - heading out by boat to Rum Point, anchoring up and meeting with friends. It gets pretty busy, but the atmosphere is buzzing, with people standing in the water next to their boat enjoying a famous Caymanian 'mud slide' cocktail or a beer and 'shooting the breeze'.

The cruise ships bring anything from 2,000 to 12,000 day trippers daily, some in search of a Rolex watch, others a cold beer, a T-shirt or a driver who can take them along the coast to Seven Mile Beach. Dive boats, jet skis and even a helicopter await visitors, depending on their budget. The water in the harbour is so clear and blue that many visitors are happy to stay around there to snorkel or dive, eat freshly chopped coconut from the street vendors, then walk along to the open-air fish market, choose a fish, take it to a local restaurant and have them cook it!

Cayman Courtesy – The Cayman Way.
Caymanians are naturally very courteous and friendly to tourists, but also to each other. This might be the Caribbean, but when it comes to good manners, Caymanians are sticklers! It is customary to always exchange pleasantries when greeting each other. The use of 'Mr', 'Mam' and 'Miss' is widespread. As a sign of respect for an elder or someone in authority, a younger Caymanian might use 'Mr' in front of someone's first name, for example 'Mr John', or 'Miss Sue'.

The Cayman Islands have developed at an incredible rate in the last few decades but it doesn't take long to see that the traditions and the 'Old Ways' are still cherished. As development increases along the azure and white shorelines, and more international businesses relocate here, Caymanians continue to take enormous pride in their heritage and constantly seek ways to protect it.

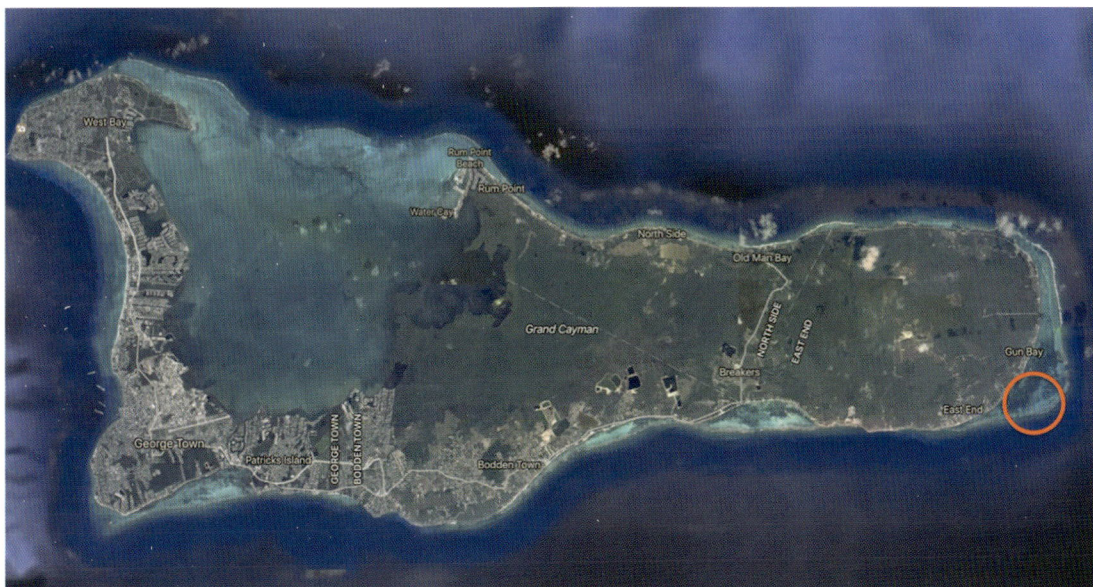

Map data: Google, DigitalGlobe

The Cayman Islands lie 480 miles south of Miami Florida and 180 miles north west of Jamaica. They are made up of three islands: Grand Cayman, the largest and most developed, the smaller sister islands Cayman Brac and Little Cayman.

The total population is over 60,000 with the majority of people living in Grand Cayman. The smaller sister islands have tiny populations - Little Cayman has less than 170 people, whilst Cayman Brac has under 2,000.

The shoreline of Gun Bay on Grand Cayman, where six small monuments commemorate those who lost their lives in the Wreck of the Ten Sail in 1794

The Author

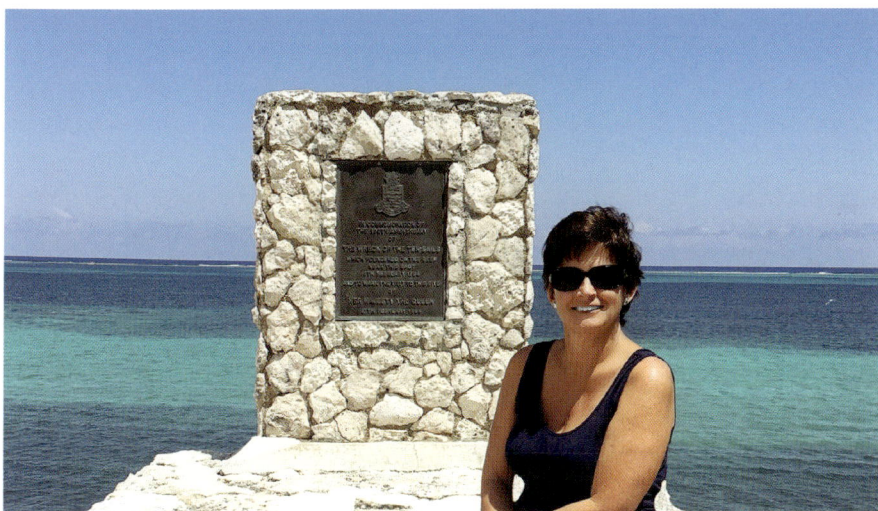

Author Sam Oakley is best known for her television presenting work with credits that include BBC *Watchdog*, *Healthcheck*, *World in Action*, *Countryfile* and the History channel. She also presented her own radio show for the BBC for many years and has worked across media and PR.

Originally from Buckinghamshire, Sam has lived in Paris and London. She is well used to island living, having spent many years living in Guernsey in the Channel Islands before making the move to the Cayman Islands with her husband and two children, Harriet and George.

Acknowledgements

It was my discovery of Dr Margaret Leshikar-Denton's excellent account of 'The Wreck of the Ten Sails' in the Cayman Islands National Archive *Our Island's Past* series that first fired my enthusiasm to delve further into the extraordinary story behind the legend that links the islands' tax-free status to the maritime disaster that occurred more than two centuries ago.

I am also indebted to numerous other local printed and on-line sources such as the very informative caymanresident.com and caymanprepared.ky, as well as the historian and author Carolyn Harris; Roger Smith's *Maritime Heritage of the Cayman Islands* and Michael Craton's *Founded Upon the Seas* among others.

I am particularly grateful to the staff at the National Archives at Kew, near London, for their kind assistance in allowing me to photograph documents relating to the loss of HMS *Convert* and for permission to reproduce some of them here. I would also like to thank Tricia Bodden and the team at the Cayman Islands National Archive for all their fantastic help.

Thanks are also due to Fidelity Bank for their kind and generous support. I would also like to thank the following: Cindy O'Hara and the team at Cayman Enterprise City; Harriet Green for her incredible contribution to the book's photography; George Town Library and Eco Rides, East End, Grand Cayman.

I must thank Jerry Johns of Polperro Heritage Press, without whom this book would never have happened. I have loved every minute working with him and have learnt a great deal in the process! Finally, thanks to my husband Nick, Harrie and George for all their encouragement and support.